Devotion to the Seven Sorrows of Mary

A Collection including the Chaplet, Prayers, Litany, Hymn and Indulgences

Edited By
J. M. Roberts, M. A.

Civitas Dei Publications
ISBN 9798591119881

Texts of the New Testament used in the work are taken from the
The Holy Bible, Douay-Rheims Version, with revisions and
footnotes (in the text in italics) by Bishop Richard Challoner, 1749-52.
Taken from a hardcopy of the 1899 Edition by the John Murphy
Company.

Introduction

Too often we neglect the garden of our souls though we know that the cultivation of a spiritual life is necessary if our ultimate goal is Heaven. We live a strange madness—fully invested in finite endeavors, and little or no time for God—with whom we hope to spend eternity. Perhaps one reason for this neglect is a sense of despair of truly being able to know Him in this life. God is immeasurable, indefinable, and beyond comprehension. God sent his Son, Jesus Christ, fully human and fully Divine, to show us the way, but we are too weak to follow. So we set the problem of salvation for later consideration, and continue a life of mundane thoughts and pursuits. This must change. Our time here runs short.

Our Lady understands the frailty of human nature and loves us as a mother loves her helpless infant. She is still here among us to draw us by baby steps to Jesus and to Heaven. At times, for example, at Fatima and Lourdes, she appears with great love to pray and to teach us how to love her Son, in preparation for our new life with Him.

Through the ages after her Assumption into Heaven, Our Blessed Mother appears, speaks to us and teaches us to pray and to prepare. Her prayers, like the Holy Rosary, are simple, and accessible to all. The Devotion to her Seven Sorrows is another remedy she strongly recommends throughout history for the healing of our souls.

Like the Holy Rosary, it easy to pray and simple to understand. It takes a very short time and will most assuredly draw the soul who prays it faithfully deeper into the mystery of the Incarnation and closer to God.

Schelte Adamszoon Bolswert. After Abraham Bloemaert. Mary Pierced by Seven Swords. Dutch. c. 1612-1615. Amsterdam, Rijksmuseum {{PD-US}}

Part I

The Chaplet of the Seven Sorrows of Mary with Passages from Sacred Scripture

The Origin of the Seven Sorrows of Mary

The devotion of the Seven Sorrows of Mary was approved by Pope Pius the VII in 1815, and the Feast day of Our Lady of Sorrows is traditionally celebrated on September 15th (the day after the Feast of the Exaltation of the Holy Cross, September 14th). Before the papal approval, this devotion was practiced for centuries. As early as the fourth century, St. Ambrose, and St. Ephrem the Syrian, whose prayer is recited by Eastern Catholics to this day, considered and meditated much on the sufferings of Mary during the life and death of her Son. Later on, according to the *Raccolta*[1], devotion to the Seven Sorrows of Mary was developed and promulgated by a group of men who later became the founders of the religious order known as the Servants of Mary or Servites:

---

[1] The Raccolta: or Collection of Indulgenced Prayers. With the Appendix of Indulgences granted by His Holiness Pius IX. from 1856 to 1866. Translated by Ambrose St. John, of the Oratory of St. Philip Neri, Birmingham.

"It was about the year 1233 that seven holy men of noble birth, by name Bonfiglio, Monaldio, Bonagiunta, Manetto, Amadeo, Uguccio, and Alessio Falconieri, withdrew from the city of Florence into the solitude of Mount Senario, receiving afterwards from the Church the appellation of the "Seven Blessed Founders." For it was in that solitude that, passing their days in the constant exercise of prayer, penitence, and other virtues, they, by a special revelation from the Blessed Virgin, instituted the Order called "Servants of Mary," taking for the object of their institution, meditation on the bitter pains she suffered in the Life, Passion, and Death of her Son Jesus, and, undertaking to promulgate this devotion amongst Christian people. One of the devout practices which they made use of for their purpose was a Chaplet or Rosary of Seven Divisions, in remembrance of the seven principal Dolours of the Blessed Virgin, which were to form the subject of the reciter's meditation according to his ability; the prayers to be said during such meditation being one Pater noster (Our Father) and seven Ave Maria's (Hail Mary's) for each division, with three more Ave Maria's (Hail Mary's) at the end of all, in honour of the tears shed by the same most holy Virgin in her Dolours.

This devout prayer, so acceptable to our most holy Sorrowful Mother, and so useful to Christian souls, was propagated throughout the Christian world by these Servants of Mary and it afterwards received much encouragement from Pope Benedict XIII."

The *Raccolta* goes on to outline the indulgence granted to those who practice this devotion. (See Appendix). St. Alphonsus Ligouri similarly explains the origin of this devotion, but adds the detail that in 1239 the seven Servite founders had a vision of Mary

"with a black garment in her hand, and told them that if they wished to please her, they should often meditate upon her dolours (sorrows)." (*Glories of Mary*)

The devotion continued to bear fruit in the hearts and lives of people over the years. Perhaps the cause of the greatest increase in popularity was a revelation to St. Bridget of Sweden (1303-1373) of gifts or graces promised by God through the Blessed Mother to those who daily practice meditating on the seven sorrows of Mary, reciting a Hail Mary for each sorrow as well.

As Mary explained to St. Bridget, the graces promises to those who practice this devotion are these:

I will grant peace to their families.

They will be enlightened about the divine mysteries.

I will console them in their pains and I will accompany them in their work.

I will give them as much as they ask for as long as it does not oppose the adorable will of my divine Son or the sanctification of their souls.

I will defend them in their spiritual battles with the infernal enemy and I will protect them at every instant of their lives.

I will visibly help them at the moment of their death; they will see the face of their Mother.

I have obtained (this grace) from my divine Son, that those who propagate this devotion to my tears and dolours, will be taken directly from this earthly life to eternal happiness, since all their sins will be forgiven and my Son and I will be their eternal consolation and joy.

The desirability of these gifts and the simplicity of the devotion continues to draw people throughout all generations from every nation of the world since its inception even to modern times.

As recently as the 1980's, of Our Lady appeared to three children in Kibeho, in Rwanda, central Africa, urging them to pray the Rosary and also the Devotion or Rosary of her Seven Sorrows. She appeared with this urgent message, also warning them to prepare for impending catastrophic times, 13 years prior to the terrible political upheaval and genocide in that region in 1994-1995, that took the lives of close to one million people. This apparition was approved by the Vatican in 2001. Mary continues to call us urgently to pray the Holy Rosary and the Devotion of her Seven Sorrows. With God's grace let us hear her voice.

Meditating on the Sorrows

The easiest way to begin to meditate on the Seven Sorrows is first, to find a quiet spot and a few minutes free from media and distractions. Consider each sorrow, while reading the Scriptural passage associated with it. If possible, imagine--picture in your mind, or look at an image of the event-- and reflect for a moment or two on some aspect of it. Then recite the Our Father and seven Hail Mary's, focusing on each sentence. You don't have to spend a long time before moving to the next sorrow. Tomorrow repeat the devotion, and perhaps consider another aspect of each event, or imagine the same more deeply. For example, consider her third sorrow: Think of the loss of the Child Jesus in the temple. How would you feel if your twelve-year-old child was missing, and you know, in fact, that something terrible is in store for him eventually, though you do not know when? You search for three days in sorrow. Imagine the terrible feeling of negligence for having lost sight of him, whom you are responsible for protecting. You fear that he is lost and possibly harmed. You don't know if you will ever see him again. You have great fear and remorse over losing sight of him. It has happened to many parents, maybe even some that you know. There are few sorrows that can equal that felt by a parent for a missing child.

To pray the Chaplet of the Seven Sorrows, meditate on each of the seven sorrows (dolours) of Mary, while saying one Our Father, and Seven Hail Mary's for each of our Lady's sorrows.

Scriptural readings provided here are useful aids to remember her sorrows, but not necessary to read, or to read in full, in order to complete the Chaplet or to gain the indulgence.

{{PD-US}}

Chaplet of The Seven Sorrows

Begin by making an act of contrition (sorrow) for one's sins. If desired, this prayer may be used:

Act of Contrition: "O my Lord, Thou who alone art most worthy of my love, behold me standing before Thy Divine Presence all in confusion at the thought of the many grievous injuries I have done Thee. I ask Thy pardon for them with my whole heart, repenting of them purely for love of Thee, and hating and loathing them above every other evil of this life, when I think of Thy infinite goodness. As I would rather have died a thousand times than have offended Thee, so now I am most firmly resolved to lose my life rather than offend Thee again. My crucified Jesus, I firmly purpose to cleanse my soul as soon as possible by Thy most Precious Blood in the Sacrament of Penance. And thou, most tender Virgin, Mother of Mercy and Refuge of sinners, do thou obtain for me the pardon of sin by virtue of thy bitter pains; whilst praying according to the mind of so many holy Pontiffs in order to obtain the indulgences granted to this thy holy Rosary, I hope thereby to obtain remission of all pains due to my sins.

The First Sorrow: The prophecy of Simeon.

Mary, Virgin Mother of my God, presented Jesus, her only Son, in the Temple, laid Him in the arms of holy aged Simeon, and heard his prophetic word, "This One shall be a sword of pain to pierce thine own heart," foretelling thereby the Passion and Death of her Son Jesus.

English: Woodcut for "Die Bibel in Bildern", 1860.
Artist: Julius Schnorr von Carolsfeld (1794-1872) (Public Domain) ((PD-US))

The Gospel according to Luke **(2: 21-35)**

"And after eight days were accomplished, that the child should be circumcised, his name was called JESUS, which was called by the angel, before he was conceived in the womb. [22] And after the days of her purification, according to the law of Moses, were accomplished, they carried him to Jerusalem, to present him to the Lord: [23] As it is written in the law of the Lord: Every male opening the womb shall be called holy to the Lord: [24] And to offer a sacrifice, according as it is written in the law of the Lord, a pair of turtledoves, or two young pigeons: [25] And behold there was a man in Jerusalem named Simeon, and this man was just and devout, waiting for the consolation of Israel; and the Holy Ghost was in him.

[26] And he had received an answer from the Holy Ghost, that he should not see death, before he had seen the Christ of the Lord. [27] And he came by the Spirit into the temple. And when his parents brought in the child Jesus, to do for him according to the custom of the law, [28] He also took him into his arms, and blessed God, and said: [29] Now thou dost dismiss thy servant, O Lord, according to thy word in peace; [30] Because my eyes have seen thy salvation,

[31] Which thou hast prepared before the face of all peoples: [32] A light to the revelation of the Gentiles, and the glory of thy people Israel. [33] And his father and mother were wondering at those things which were spoken concerning him.

[34] And Simeon blessed them, and said to Mary his mother: Behold this child is set for the fall, and for the resurrection of many in Israel, and for a sign which shall be contradicted; [35] And thy own soul a sword shall pierce, that, out of many hearts, thoughts may be revealed."

Recite one Our Father:

Our Father, Who art in heaven,
Hallowed be Thy Name.
Thy Kingdom come.
Thy Will be done,
on earth as it is in Heaven.
Give us this day our daily bread.
And forgive us our trespasses,
as we forgive those who trespass against us.
And lead us not into temptation,
but deliver us from evil. Amen.

Recite seven Hail Mary's:

Hail Mary,
Full of Grace,
The Lord is with thee.
Blessed art thou among women,
and blessed is the fruit
of thy womb, Jesus.
Holy Mary,
Mother of God,
pray for us sinners now,
and at the hour of our death. Amen

+++

The Second Sorrow: The flight into

Egypt. Mary was obliged to fly into Egypt by reason of the persecution of cruel Herod, who impiously sought to slay her well-beloved Son.

The Flight into Egypt | url=https://clevelandart.org/art/1959.99.14 | author=Albrecht Dürer | year=c. 1503-1505 | access-date=07 January 2021 | publisher=Cleveland Museum of Art. (Public Domain) {{PD-US}}

The Gospel according to St. Matthew 2: 1-23

"[1] When Jesus therefore was born in Bethlehem of Juda, in the days of king Herod, behold, there came wise men from the east to Jerusalem. [2] Saying, Where is he that is born king of the Jews? For we have seen his star in the east, and are come to adore him. [3] And king Herod hearing this, was troubled, and all Jerusalem with him. [4] And assembling together all the chief priests and the scribes of the people, he inquired of them where Christ should be born. [5] But they said to him: In Bethlehem of Juda. For so it is written by the prophet:

[6] And thou Bethlehem the land of Juda art not the least among the princes of Juda: for out of thee shall come forth the captain that shall rule my people Israel. [7] Then Herod, privately calling the wise men, learned diligently of them the time of the star which appeared to them; [8] And sending them into Bethlehem, said: Go and diligently inquire after the child, and when you have found him, bring me word again, that I also may come to adore him. [9] Who having heard the king, went their way; and behold the star which they had seen in the east, went before them, until it came and stood over where the child was. [10] And seeing the star they rejoiced with exceeding great joy.

[11] And entering into the house, they found the child with Mary his mother, and falling down they adored him; and opening their treasures, they offered him gifts; gold, frankincense, and myrrh. [12] And having received an answer in sleep that they should not return to Herod, they went back another way into their country. [13] And after they were departed, behold an angel of the Lord appeared in sleep to Joseph, saying: Arise, and take the child and his mother, and fly into Egypt: and be there until I shall tell thee. For it will come to pass that Herod will seek the child to destroy him. [14] Who arose, and took the child and his mother by night, and retired into Egypt: and he was there until the death of Herod: [15] That it might be fulfilled which the Lord spoke by the prophet, saying: Out of Egypt have I called my son.[16] Then Herod perceiving that he was deluded by the wise men, was exceeding angry; and sending killed all the men children that were in Bethlehem, and in all the borders thereof, from two years old and under, according to the time which he had diligently inquired of the wise men. [17] Then was fulfilled that which was spoken by Jeremias the prophet, saying: [18] A voice in Rama was heard, lamentation and great mourning; Rachel bewailing her children, and would not be comforted, because they are not. [19] But when Herod was dead, behold an angel of the Lord appeared in sleep to Joseph in Egypt, [20]

Saying: Arise, and take the child and his mother, and go into the land of Israel. For they are dead that sought the life of the child.

[21] Who arose, and took the child and his mother, and came into the land of Israel. [22] But hearing that Archelaus reigned in Judea in the room of Herod his father, he was afraid to go thither: and being warned in sleep retired into the quarters of Galilee. [23] And coming he dwelt in a city called Nazareth: that it might be fulfilled which was said by prophets: That he shall be called a Nazarene."

Recite one Our Father:

Our Father, Who art in heaven,
Hallowed be Thy Name.
Thy Kingdom come.
Thy Will be done,
on earth as it is in Heaven.
Give us this day our daily bread.
And forgive us our trespasses,
as we forgive those who trespass against us.
And lead us not into temptation,
but deliver us from evil. Amen.

Recite seven Hail Mary's:

Hail Mary,
Full of Grace,
The Lord is with thee.
Blessed art thou among women,
and blessed is the fruit
of thy womb, Jesus.
Holy Mary,
Mother of God,
pray for us sinners now,
and at the hour of our death. Amen

+++

The Third Sorrow: The loss of the Child Jesus in the temple. Mary, after having gone up to Jerusalem at the Paschal Feast with Joseph her spouse and Jesus her dear Son, lost Him on her return to her poor house, and for three days bewailed the loss of her beloved Son.

Jesus converses with the learned ones in the Temple. Gustave Doré (1832–1883) Blue pencil.svg. Public Domain USA. ((PD-US))

The Gospel according to St. Luke 2: 43-45

"[40] And the child grew, and waxed strong, full of wisdom; and the grace of God was in him. [41] And his parents went every year to Jerusalem, at the solemn day of the pasch, [42] And when he was twelve years old, they going up into Jerusalem, according to the custom of the feast, [43] And having fulfilled the days, when they returned, the child Jesus remained in Jerusalem; and his parents knew it not. [44] And thinking that he was in the company, they came a day's journey, and sought him among their kinsfolks and acquaintance. [45] And not finding him, they returned into Jerusalem, seeking him.

[46] And it came to pass, that, after three days, they found him in the temple, sitting in the midst of the doctors, hearing them, and asking them questions. [47] And all that heard him were astonished at his wisdom and his answers. [48] And seeing him, they wondered. And his mother said to him: Son, why hast thou done so to us? behold thy father and I have sought thee sorrowing. [49] And he said to them: How is it that you sought me? did you not know, that I must be about my father's business? [50] And they understood not the word that he spoke unto them.

[51] And he went down with them, and came to Nazareth, and was subject to them. And his mother kept all these words in her heart. [52] And Jesus advanced in wisdom, and age, and grace with God and men."

Recite one Our Father:

Our Father, Who art in heaven,
Hallowed be Thy Name.
Thy Kingdom come.
Thy Will be done,
on earth as it is in Heaven.
Give us this day our daily bread.
And forgive us our trespasses,
as we forgive those who trespass against us.
And lead us not into temptation,
but deliver us from evil. Amen.

Recite seven Hail Mary's:

Hail Mary,
Full of Grace,
The Lord is with thee.
Blessed art thou among women,
and blessed is the fruit
of thy womb, Jesus.
Holy Mary,
Mother of God,
pray for us sinners now,
and at the hour of our death. Amen

+++

The Fourth Sorrow: Mary met her dear Son Jesus carrying on His tender shoulders the heavy cross whereon He was to be crucified for our salvation.

Christ Carrying the Cross, from The Passion. 1512. Engraving. Albrecht Dürer (German, Nuremberg 1471–1528) (Public Domainn) ((PD-US))

The Gospel according to St. Luke 23: 27-32.

"[27] And there followed him a great multitude of people, and of women, who bewailed and lamented him. [28] But Jesus turning to them, said: Daughters of Jerusalem, weep not over me; but weep for yourselves, and for your children. [29] For behold, the days shall come, wherein they will say: Blessed are the barren, and the wombs that have not borne, and the paps that have not given suck. [30] Then shall they begin to say to the mountains: Fall upon us; and to the hills: Cover us.

[31] For if in the green wood they do these things, what shall be done in the dry?"

Recite one Our Father:

Our Father, Who art in heaven,
Hallowed be Thy Name.
Thy Kingdom come.
Thy Will be done,
on earth as it is in Heaven.
Give us this day our daily bread.
And forgive us our trespasses,
as we forgive those who trespass against us.
And lead us not into temptation,
but deliver us from evil. Amen.

Recite seven Hail Mary's:

Hail Mary,
Full of Grace,
The Lord is with thee.
Blessed art thou among women,
and blessed is the fruit
of thy womb, Jesus.
Holy Mary,
Mother of God,
pray for us sinners now,
and at the hour of our death. Amen

+++

The Fifth Sorrow: Mary saw her Son Jesus raised upon the tree of the cross, and Blood pouring forth from every part of His Sacred Body; and when then, after three long hours' agony, she beheld Him die.

Crucifixion. 1508. Albrecht Dürer. German. 1471-1528 (Public Domain){(PD-US)}

The Crucifixion and Death of Jesus
The Gospel according to St. John 19: 25-27:

"[25] Now there stood by the cross of Jesus, his mother, and his mother's sister, Mary of Cleophas, and Mary Magdalen.

[26] When Jesus therefore had seen his mother and the disciple standing whom he loved, he saith to his mother: Woman, behold thy son. [27] After that, he saith to the disciple: Behold thy mother. And from that hour, the disciple took her to his own."

Recite one Our Father:

Our Father, Who art in heaven,
Hallowed be Thy Name.
Thy Kingdom come.
Thy Will be done,
on earth as it is in Heaven.
Give us this day our daily bread.
And forgive us our trespasses,
as we forgive those who trespass against us.
And lead us not into temptation,
but deliver us from evil. Amen.

Recite seven Hail Mary's:

Hail Mary,
Full of Grace,
The Lord is with thee.
Blessed art thou among women,
and blessed is the fruit
of thy womb, Jesus.
Holy Mary,
Mother of God,
pray for us sinners now,
and at the hour of our death. Amen

+++

The Sixth Sorrow: Jesus is removed from the cross. Mary saw the lance cleave the Sacred Side of Jesus, her beloved Son, and when taken down from the cross, His Holy Body was laid in her purest bosom.

The Descent from the Cross, from The Small Passion. Albrecht Dürer (German, Nuremberg 1471-1528 Nuremberg) Date: ca. 1509. Woodcut. (Public Domain) ((PD-US))

The Gospel According to John (19: 28-38)
"Afterwards, Jesus knowing that all things were now accomplished, that the scripture might be fulfilled, said: I thirst. [29] Now there was a vessel set there full of vinegar. And they, putting a sponge full of vinegar and hyssop, put it to his mouth. [30] Jesus therefore, when he had taken the vinegar, said: It is consummated. And bowing his head, he gave up the ghost.[31] Then the Jews, (because it was the parasceve,) that the bodies might not remain on the cross on the sabbath day, (for that was a great sabbath day,) besought Pilate that their legs might be broken, and that they might be taken away. [32] The soldiers therefore came; and they broke the legs of the first, and of the other that was crucified with him. [33] But after they were come to Jesus, when they saw that he was already dead, they did not break his legs. [34] But one of the soldiers with a spear opened his side, and immediately there came out blood and water. [35] And he that saw it, hath given testimony, and his testimony is true. And he knoweth that he saith true; that you also may believe.[36] For these things were done, that the scripture might be fulfilled: You shall not break a bone of him. [37] And again another scripture saith: They shall look on him whom they pierced. [38] And after these things, Joseph of Arimathea (because he was a disciple of Jesus, but secretly for fear of the Jews) besought Pilate that he might take

away the body of Jesus. And Pilate gave leave. He came therefore, and took the body of Jesus. [39] And Nicodemus also came, (he who at the first came to Jesus by night,) bringing a mixture of myrrh and aloes, about an hundred pound weight. [40] They took therefore the body of Jesus, and bound it in linen cloths, with the spices, as the manner of the Jews is to bury."

Recite one Our Father:

Our Father, Who art in heaven,
Hallowed be Thy Name.
Thy Kingdom come.
Thy Will be done,
on earth as it is in Heaven.
Give us this day our daily bread.
And forgive us our trespasses,
as we forgive those who trespass against us.
And lead us not into temptation,
but deliver us from evil. Amen.

Recite seven Hail Mary's:

Hail Mary,
Full of Grace,
The Lord is with thee.
Blessed art thou among women,
and blessed is the fruit
of thy womb, Jesus.
Holy Mary,
Mother of God,
pray for us sinners now,
and at the hour of our death. Amen

+++

The Seventh Sorrow: The Burial of Jesus.

The last sorrow of the Blessed Virgin, Queen and Advocate of us her servants, miserable sinners, was when she saw the Holy Body of her Son buried in the grave.

The Entombment, from "The Passion of Christ" Hendrick Goltzius (Netherlandish. Mühlbracht 1558–1617 Haarlem) Date: 1596. Engraving. (((PD-US)))

The Burial of Jesus. The Gospel According to St. Luke (23: 46-56)

[46] "And Jesus crying out with a loud voice, said: Father, into thy hands I commend my spirit. And saying this, he gave up the ghost. [47] Now the centurion, seeing what was done, glorified God, saying: Indeed this was a just man. [48] And all the multitude of them that were come together to that sight, and saw the things that were done, returned striking their breasts. [49] And all his acquaintance, and the women that had followed him from Galilee, stood afar off, beholding these things. [50] And behold there was a man named Joseph, who was a counsellor, a good and just man, [51] (The same had not consented to their counsel and doings;) of Arimathea, a city of Judea; who also himself looked for the kingdom of God. [52] This man went to Pilate, and begged the body of Jesus. [53] And taking him down, he wrapped him in fine linen, and laid him in a sepulchre that was hewed in stone, wherein never yet any man had been laid. [54] And it was the day of the Parasceve, and the sabbath drew on. [55] And the women that were come with him from Galilee, following after, saw the sepulchre, and how his body was laid.

[56] And returning, they prepared spices and ointments; and on the sabbath day they rested, according to the commandment."

Recite one Our Father:

Our Father, Who art in heaven,
Hallowed be Thy Name.
Thy Kingdom come.
Thy Will be done,
on earth as it is in Heaven.
Give us this day our daily bread.
And forgive us our trespasses,
as we forgive those who trespass against us.
And lead us not into temptation,
but deliver us from evil. Amen.

Recite seven Hail Mary's:

Hail Mary,
Full of Grace,
The Lord is with thee.
Blessed art thou among women,
and blessed is the fruit
of thy womb, Jesus.
Holy Mary,
Mother of God,
pray for us sinners now,
and at the hour of our death. Amen

Concluding Prayer of the Chaplet of the Seven Sorrows

At the end, say three Hail Mary's in veneration of the tears which Mary shed in her sorrows, to obtain thereby true sorrow for sins and the holy Indulgences attached to this pious exercise.

V. Pray for us, Virgin most sorrowful.

R. That we may be made worthy of the promises of Christ.

Let us pray.

Grant, we beseech Thee, O Lord Jesus Christ, that the most blessed Virgin Mary, Thy Mother, may intercede for us before the throne of Thy mercy, now and at the hour of our death, whose most holy soul was transfixed with the sword of sorrow in the hour of Thine own Passion. Through Thee, Jesus Christ, Saviour of the world, who livest and reignest with the Father and the Holy Ghost for ever and ever. Amen.

Part   II

Prayers, Hymns and Devotions to Our
Lady of Sorrow

Georgio Ghisi. Mater Dolorosa Surrounded by the Seven Sorrows. Italian, c. 1575. Philadelphia, Museum of Art. ((PD-US))

Prayer to Our Lady of Kibeho

Blessed Virgin Mary, Mother of the Word, Mother of all those who believe in Him and who welcome Him into their lives, we are here before you to contemplate you. We believe that you are amongst us, like a mother in the midst of her children, even though we do not see you with our bodily eyes.

We bless you, the sure way that leads us to Jesus the Savior, for all the favors which you endlessly pour out upon us, especially that, in your meekness, you were gracious enough to appear miraculously in Kibeho, just when our world needed it most.

Grant us always the light and strength necessary to accept, will all seriousness, your call to us to be converted, to repent, and to live according to your Son's Gospel. Teach us how to pray with sincerity, and to love one another as He loved us, so that, just as you have requested, we may always be beautiful flowers diffusing their pleasant fragrance everywhere and upon everyone.

Holy Mary, Our Lady of Sorrows, teach us to understand the value of the cross in our lives, so that whatever is still lacking to the sufferings of Christ we may fill up in our own bodies for His mystical Body, which is the Church.

And, when our pilgrimage on this earth comes to an end, may we live eternally with you in the kingdom of Heaven. Amen. (reprinted from: **https://denvercatholic.org/our-lady-of-kibehos-message-to-the-world/**)

ONE HOUR'S PRAYER IN THE YEAR.[2]
(*Raccolta # 98.*)

Pope Clement XII., by a decree of the Sacred Congregation of Indulgences, February 4, 1736, and Benedict XIV., by another decree of July 14, 1757, granted:

A plenary indulgence once in the year to all the faithful who on any one day should, after Confession and Communion, make one hour's prayer in honour of the sorrows of most holy Mary, calling them to mind by saying the Chaplet of them, or other prayers adapted to this devotion. Pope Pius VI., of blessed memory, renewed this Indulgence and confirmed it for ever, July 8, 1785.

---

[2] The following are taken from the *Raccolta*. , Nos. 98-102.

EXERCISE IN HONOUR OF HER SORROWFUL HEART. (*Raccolta #99.*)

Pope Pius VII., at the prayer of the priests of the Pious Union of the Sacred Heart of Jesus, sometimes called "Pious Union of St. Paul" (already several times referred to above), granted, by a Rescript of Jan. 14, 1815, issued through the Archbishop of Philippi, at that time vicegerent here in Rome, and kept in the Segretaria of his Eminence the Cardinal-Vicar -

An indulgence of 300 days to all Christians every time they say with devotion the following pious exercise in honour of the sorrowing heart of most Holy Mary.

THE EXERCISE.

V. O God, come to my assistance.

R. O Lord, make haste to help me.

Glory be to the Father, and to the Son and to the Holy Spirit, as it was in the beginning, is now and ever shall be, world without end. Amen.

i. I compassionate thee, sorrowing Mary, in the affliction of thy tender heart when the holy old man Simeon prophesied to thee. Dear Mother, by thy heart then so afflicted, obtain for me the virtue of humility and the gift of holy fear of God.

Hail Mary.

ii. I compassionate thee, sorrowing Mary, in the anxiety which thy sensitive heart underwent in the flight to and sojourn in Egypt. Dear Mother, by thy heart which was then made so anxious, obtain for me the virtue of liberality, specially towards the poor, and the gift of piety.

Ave Maria.

iii. I compassionate thee, sorrowing Mary, in the trouble of thy careful heart when thou didst lose thy dear Son Jesus. Dear Mother, by thy heart then so troubled, obtain for me the virtue of holy chastity and the gift of knowledge.

Ave Maria.

iv. I compassionate thee, sorrowing Mary, in the shock thy maternal heart underwent when Jesus met thee as He carried His cross. Dear Mother, by thy loving heart then so overwhelmed, obtain for me the virtue of patience and the gift of fortitude.

Ave Maria.

v. I compassionate thee, sorrowing Mary, in the martyrdom thy generous heart bore so nobly whilst thou didst stand by Jesus in His agony. Dear Mother, by thy heart then so martyred, obtain for me the virtue of temperance and the gift of counsel.

Hail Mary.

vi. I compassionate thee, sorrowing Mary, in the wound of thy tender heart when the sacred Side of Jesus was pierced with the lance. Dear Mother, by thy heart then so transfixed, obtain for me the virtue of fraternal charity and the gift of understanding.

Hail Mary.

vii. I compassionate thee, sorrowing Mary, in the pang felt by thy loving heart when the Body of Jesus was buried in the grave. Dear Mother, by all the bitterness of desolation thou didst then experience, obtain for me the virtue of diligence and the gift of wisdom.

Hail Mary.

V. Pray for us, Virgin most sorrowful.

R. That we may be made worthy of the promises of Christ.

Let us pray.

Grant, we beseech Thee, O Lord Jesus Christ, that the most blessed Virgin Mary, Thy Mother, may intercede for us before the throne of Thy mercy, now and at the hour of our death, whose most holy soul was transfixed with the sword of sorrow in the hour of Thine own Passion. Through Thee, Jesus Christ, Saviour of the world, who livest and reignest with the Father and the Holy Ghost for ever and ever. Amen.

Vicente Aznar, Our Lady of Sorrows. Spanish, 19th Century. Madrid, Biblioteca Nacional de España ((PD-US))

SEVEN "HAIL MARY'S" AND SEVEN "Holy Mother's" etc. ("SANCTA MATER'S") *(Raccolta #100)*

Pope Pius VII., by a Brief of Dec. 1, 1815, in order to augment in all the faithful devotion towards the sorrows of most holy Mary, and the more to excite in them grateful recollections of the Passion of her Son, Jesus, granted:

i. A 300 days indulgence, once a day, to all who, contrite in heart, shall say seven Hail Mary's, with the versicle to each:

"Holy Mother, pierce me through;
In my heart each wound renew
Of thy Saviour crucified."(from the *Stabat Mater)*

ii. A plenary indulgence, once every month, and remission of all sins, to all who should have devoutly practiced this pious exercise for a month together, on any one day when, after Confession and Communion, they shall pray for the Holy Church, &c.

This Brief is kept in the Capitular Archivium of the cathedral of Arezze, whose bishop made prayer to the Holy Father for the Indulgence.

Pope Pius VII., in order to augment the devotion of the faithful towards the Sacred Heart of Mary Sorrowing, and at the same time to make some compensations for the many offences which are committed against God on the days of the carnival, granted by a Rescript given through the Segretaria of the Memorials, Dec. 9, I815, and kept in the Segretaria of his Eminence the Cardinal-Vicar -

i. A 300 days' indulgence, to all the faithful of the Catholic world, every time they shall assist at any devout exercise in honour of the Sorrows of most holy Mary, on the ten last days of the carnival, in any church or public oratory, or in any church of regulars of either sex, or in any oratory or chapel in monasteries, seminaries, or other pious places where prayer is wont to be made.

ii. A plenary indulgence, to those who shall assist at this pious exercise for at least five out of the ten days; provided that on one of the ten days, they, after Confession and Communion, pray to God for the Holy Church, &c.

These Indulgences were confirmed for ever by the same Pius VII., through the S. Congregation of Indulgences, June 18, 1822.

+++

Novena Prayer to Our Lady of Sorrows

(Repeat this prayer for nine consecutive days.)

I grieve for you, Mary most sorrowful, in the consternation of your heart at meeting Jesus as He carried His cross. Dear Mother, by your heart so troubled, obtain for me the virtue of patience and the gift of fortitude. (Recite one Hail Mary)

V. Pray for us, O Virgin most sorrowful.
R. That we may be made worthy of the promises of Christ.

THE HOUR OR HALF-HOUR OF PRAYER ON GOOD FRIDAY AND OTHER FRIDAYS. (*Raccolta #102*)

In order to engage the faithful to endeavour to give an increase of consolation to most holy Mary in her desolation, Pius VII., by two Rescripts given through the Segretaria of the Memorials, Feb. 25 and March 21, 1815, kept in the Segretaria of his Eminence the Cardinal-Vicar, granted:

i. A plenary indulgence to all those who, from three o'clock on Good Friday until midday on Holy Saturday (the hour on that day when the Holy Church invites the faithful to rejoice in the Resurrection of Jesus Christ), shall, either in public or in private, keep one hour, or at least half an hour, in honour of most holy Mary in desolation, by meditating on her seven dolours, saying the Chaplet of her Dolours, or any other prayers having reference to her desolation. This Indulgence is gained when, by Confessions and Communions, they satisfy the precept of Paschal Communion.

ii. An indulgence of 300 days, on other Fridays whenever between three o'clock on that day and the dawn of Sunday, they practice this devotion.

iii. A plenary indulgence each month to all who have practiced it every week in the month, provided that they go to Confession and Communion on one of the last days of the devotion.

All these Indulgences were Confirmed by the same Pope Pius VII. forever, through the S. Congregation of Indulgences, June 18, 1822.

SHORT PRAYER TO THE MOST HOLY VIRGIN IN HER DESOLATION. (*Raccolta* #103)

His Holiness Pope Pius IX., by a decree of the S. Congr. of Indulgences, of Dec. 23, 1847, deigned to grant:

An indulgence of 100 days to all the faithful, every time they say with contrite heart the following prayer in honour of the most holy Virgin in her desolation:

Hail Mary, full of sorrows, the Crucified is with thee: tearful art thou amongst women, and tearful is the fruit of thy womb, Jesus. Holy Mary, Mother of the Crucified, grant tears to us crucifiers of thy Son, now and at the hour of our death. Amen.

Litany of Our Lady of Seven Sorrows

Lord, have mercy on us.

Christ, have mercy on us.

Lord, have mercy on us.

Christ, hear us.

Christ, graciously hear us.

God, the Father of heaven, Have mercy on us.

God the Son, Redeemer of the world, Have mercy on us.

God the Holy Ghost, Have mercy on us.

Holy Mary, Mother of God, pray for us.

Holy Virgin of virgins, pray for us.

Mother of the Crucified, pray for us.

Sorrowful Mother, pray for us.

Mournful Mother, pray for us.

Sighing Mother, pray for us.

Afflicted Mother, pray for us.

Forsaken Mother, pray for us.

Desolate Mother, pray for us.

Mother most sad, pray for us.

Mother set around with anguish, pray for us.

Mother overwhelmed by grief, pray for us.

Mother transfixed by a sword, pray for us.
Mother crucified in thy heart, pray for us.
Mother bereaved of thy Son, pray for us.
Sighing Dove, pray for us.
Mother of Dolours, pray for us.
Fount of tears, pray for us.
Sea of bitterness, pray for us.
Field of tribulation, pray for us.
Mass of suffering, pray for us.
Mirror of patience, pray for us.
Rock of constancy, pray for us.
Remedy in perplexity, pray for us.
Joy of the afflicted, pray for us.
Ark of the desolate, pray for us.
Refuge of the abandoned, pray for us.
Shield of the oppressed, pray for us.
Conqueror of the incredulous, pray for us.
Solace of the wretched, pray for us.
Medicine of the sick, pray for us.
Help of the faint, pray for us.
Strength of the weak, pray for us.
Protectress of those who fight, pray for us.
Haven of the shipwrecked, pray for us.
Calmer of tempests, pray for us.
Companion of the sorrowful, pray for us.
Retreat of those who groan, pray for us.
Terror of the treacherous, pray for us.
Standard-bearer of the Martyrs, pray for us.
Treasure of the Faithful, pray for us.
Light of Confessors, pray for us.
Pearl of Virgins, pray for us.

Comfort of Widows, pray for us.

Joy of all Saints, pray for us.

Queen of thy Servants, pray for us.

Holy Mary, who alone art unexampled, pray for us.

Pray for us, most Sorrowful Virgin,

That we may be made worthy of the promises of Christ.

O God, in whose Passion, according to the prophecy of Simeon, a sword of grief pierced through the most sweet soul of Thy glorious Blessed Virgin Mother Mary: grant that we, who celebrate the memory of her Seven Sorrows, may obtain the happy effect of Thy Passion, Who lives and reigns world without end. Amen.

Pope Pius VII. From *The Servite Manual*

A Prayer to the Most Holy Virgin Mother of Sorrows

Mary, Virgin, Mother of God, Martyr of love and sorrow, because thou didst witness the pains and torments of Jesus: truly didst thou concur in the great work of my redemption, first, by thine innumerable afflictions, and then by the offering thou didst make to the Eternal Father of His and thine only-begotten, as a holocaust and victim of propitiation for my sins. I compassionate thee for the bitter pain which thou didst suffer. I thank thee for that love, well-nigh infinite, through which thou didst bereave thyself of the Fruit of the womb, true God, and true man, to save me, a sinner; let thine intercession be ever interposed with the Father and the Son for me, that I may steadily amend my evil ways, and never, by further faults, crucify afresh my loving Saviour; that so, persevering in His grace until death, I may obtain eternal life: through the merits of His dolorous Passion and His death upon the Cross.

Say: Three Hail Mary's

Let Us Pray.

O Lord Jesus Christ, Who, at the sixth hour of the day, didst, for the Redemption of the world, mount the gibbet of the Cross, and shed Thy precious Blood for the remission of sins; we humbly beseech Thee to grant us, after our death, a joyful entrance into the gates of paradise. Grant, we beseech Thee, O Lord Jesus Christ, that now, and at the hour of our death, the Blessed Mary, ever Virgin, Thy Mother, may intercede for us, through whose most holy soul a sword passed in the hour of Thy Passion: through Thee, Jesus Christ, Saviour of the world, Who, with the Father and the Holy Ghost livest and reignest forever and ever.

Amen.

+++

Feast Day of Our Lady of Sorrows

This feast is traditionally celebrated in the Church on September 15th, the day after the feast of the Holy Cross, September 14th. It is an excellent day for praying the consecration to Our Lady of Sorrows.

Consecration to Our Lady of Sorrows

Most holy Virgin and Queen of Martyrs, Mary, would that I could be in Heaven, there to contemplate the honors rendered to thee by the Most Holy Trinity and by the whole Heavenly Court! But since I am still a pilgrim in this vale of tears, receive from me, thy unworthy servant and a poor sinner, the most sincere homage and the most perfect act of vassalage a human creature can offer thee. In thy Immaculate Heart, pierced with so many swords of sorrow, I place today my poor soul forever; receive me as a partaker in thy dolours, and never suffer that I should depart from that Cross on which thy only begotten Son expired for me. With thee, O Mary, I will endure all the sufferings, contradictions, infirmities, with which it will please thy Divine Son to visit me in this life. All of them I offer to thee, in memory of the Dolours which thou didst suffer during thy life, that every thought of my mind, every beating of my heart may henceforward be an act of compassion to thy Sorrows, and of complacency for the glory thou now enjoyest in Heaven. Since then, O Dear Mother, I now compassionate thy Dolours, and rejoice in seeing thee glorified, do thou also have compassion on me, and reconcile me to thy Son Jesus, that I may become thy true and loyal son (daughter); come on my last day and assist me in my last agony, even as thou wert present at the Agony of thy Divine Son Jesus, that from this painful exile I may go to Heaven, there to be made partaker of thy glory. Amen.

THE MONTH OF SEPTEMBER; OR CONSIDERATIONS AND DEVOUT AFFECTIONS UPON THE DOLOURS OF MOST HOLY MARY *(Raccolta. #178 Appendix)*

By a Brief of April 3, 1857, his Holiness Pope Pius IX. Granted:

300 days indulgence, to be gained on any day in the month of September by all the faithful who, with contrition of heart, shall practice this devout exercise for the month of September, dedicated to the Dolours of most holy Mary, on condition of their making use of the following little book, entitled The Month of September; or Considerations and Devout Affections upon the Dolours of most holy Mary; adapted to the use of every one who is devoted to this same Mother of God, &c. It is reprinted at the press of Baldassari, at Rome, under the date of the year 1857, and is on sale at the shop of Joseph Ossani, No. 21A, in the street of the Pie di Marmo.

Hymn to the Sorrowing Mother of Christ[3]

(**Note:** The following is taken from the *Raccolta: or Collection of Indulgenced Prayers. With Appendix of Indulgences granted by His Holiness Pius IX. From 1856-1866.* Translated by Ambrose St. John, of the Oratory of St. Philip Neri, Birmingham.)

THE HYMN "STABAT MATER."

The venerable Pope Innocent XI., desirous that all faithful Christians should often call to mind the bitter sorrow endured by most holy Mary whilst she stood beneath the cross of her divine Son Jesus, entreating her through that great sorrow of hers to obtain for them spiritual favours in their life and in their death, - granted, by his Brief, Commissae nobis, of Sept. 1, 1681 -An indulgence of 100 days to all the faithful every time that, in honour of the sorrow of the B. V. Mary, they devoutly say the sequence or hymn Stabat Mater; a hymn which,[4] though not composed by St. Gregory the Great or St. Bonaventure, as some suppose, yet acknowledges for its author the learned Pope Innocent III., as attested by many writers of great authority.

---

[3] (**Note:** Quoted from the *Raccolta: or Collection of Indulgenced Prayers. With Appendix of Indulgences granted by His Holiness Pius IX. From 1856-1866.* Translated by Ambrose St. John, of the Oratory of St. Philip Neri, Birmingham.)

[4] Benedict XIV. on the Feasts of our Lord and B.V.M. Part ii. cap. iv. § 1, at the end

STABAT MATER

The authorship of this beautiful hymn or poem is not known with certainty, but is often attributed to the Franciscan Jacopone da Todi, (1230-1306). It has been set to music by many great composers. It is traditionally sung during Lent, while praying the Stations of the Cross.

Stabat Mater dolorosa Juxta crucem lacrymosa Dum pendebat Filius.	At the cross her station keeping, Stood the mournful Mother weeping, Close to Jesus to the last;
Cujus animam gementern,Contristatam et dolentem, Pertransivit gladius.	Through her heart, His sorrow sharing, All His bitter anguish bearing, Now at length the sword had passed.
O quam tristis et afflicta Fuit illa benedicta Mater Unigeniti!	O, how sad and sore distressed Was that Mother, highly blest, Of the sole-begotten One!
Quae moerebat, et dolebat, Illa Mater dum videbat Nati poenas incliti. Quis est homo qui non fleret,Matrem Christi si videret In tanto supplicio?	Christ above in torment hangs; She beneath beholds the pangs Of her dying glorious Son. Is there one who would not weep,'Whelmed in miseries so deep Christ's dear Mother to behold?
Quis non posset contristari Christi Matrem contemplari Dolentem cum Filio. Pro peccatis suae gentis Vidit Jesum in tormentis,	Can the human heart refrain From partaking in her pain, In that Mother's pain untold. Bruised, derided, cursed, defiled, She beheld her tender child, All with bloody scourges

Et flagellis subditum.	rent; For the sins of His own nation
Visit suum dulcem Natum Moriendo desolatum, Dum emisit Spiritum.	Saw Him hang in desolationTill His Spirit forth He sent.
Eja Mater, fons amoris,Me sentire vim doloris Fac, ut tecum lugeam.	O thou Mother! Fount of love! Touch my spirit from above, Make my heart with thine accord; Make me feel as thou hast felt;
Fac, ut ardeat cor meum In amando Christum Deum, Ut sibi complaceam.	Make my soul to glow and melt With the love of Christ my Lord.
Sancta Mater istud agas, Crucifixi fige plagas Cordi meo valide. Tui Nati vulnerati,Tam dignati pro me pati, Poenas mecum divide.	Holy Mother! pierce me through; In my heart each wound renew Of my Saviour crucified; Let me share with thee His pain, Who for all my sins was slain, Who for me in torment died.
Fac me tecum pie flere, Crucifixo condolere, Donec ego vixero.	Let me mingle tears with thee, Mourning Him who mourned for me, All the days that I may live:
Juxta crucem tecum stare, Et me tibi sociare In planctu desidero.	By the cross with thee to stay; There with thee to weep and pray, Is all I ask of thee to give.
Virgo virginum praeclara Mihi jam non sis amara, Fac me tecum plangere. Fac, ut portem Christi mortem,	Virgin of all virgins best! Listen to my fond request: Let me share thy grief divine; Let me to my latest breath In my body bear the deathOf that dying Son of thine.
Passionis fac consortem,	Wounded with His every

Et plagas recolere.
Fac me plagis vulnerari,
Fac me cruce inebriari,
Et cruore Filii.

Flammis ne urar succensus,
Per te, Virgo, sim defensus,
In die judicii.Christe, cum sit
hinc exire,
Da per Matrem me venire Ad
patrem victoriae.

Quando corpus morietur, Fac
ut animae donetur Paradisi
gloria. Amen.

wound,Steep my soul till it
hath swooned
In His very Blood away;
Be to me, O Virgin, nigh,
Lest in flames I burn and die
In His awful judgment-day.
Christ, when Thou shalt call
me hence,Be Thy Mother my
defence, Be Thy cross my
victory.

While my body here decays,
May my soul Thy goodness
praise Safe in Paradise with
Thee. Amen

Jacob Corneliszoon, Mary Pierced by a Sword. From *Die Kleine Passion* (Page 45). Dutch. c. 1520-1521. Dresden, Kupferstich-Kabinett. Public Domain. {{PD-US}}

Feasts of the Seven Sorrows of the Blessed Virgin Mary. (According to the *Catholic Encyclopedia*[5]**)** There are two such days: Friday before Palm Sunday, major double; third Sunday in September double of the second class. The object of these feasts is the spiritual martyrdom of the Mother of God and her compassion with the sufferings of her Divine Son. (1) The seven founders of the Servite Order, in 1239, five years after they established themselves on Monte Senario, took up the sorrows of Mary, standing under the Cross, as the principal devotion of their order. The corresponding feast, however, did not originate with them; its celebration was enacted by a provincial synod of Cologne (1413) to expiate the crimes of the iconoclast Hussites; it was to be kept on the Friday after the third Sunday after Easter under the title: "Commemoratio augustix et doloris B. Marix V.". Its object was exclusively the sorrow of Mary during the Crucifixion and Death of Christ. Before the sixteenth century this

---

[5] Holweck, Frederick. "Feasts of the Seven Sorrows of the Blessed Virgin Mary." The Catholic Encyclopedia. Vol. 14. New York: Robert Appleton Company, 1912.

Ecclesiastical approbation. Nihil Obstat. July 1, 1912. Remy Lafort, S.T.D., Censor. Imprimatur. +John Cardinal Farley, Archbishop of New York.

feast was limited to the dioceses of North Germany, Scandinavia, and Scotland. Being termed "Compassio" or "Transfixio", "Commendatio, Lamentatio B.M.V.", it was kept at a great variety of dates, mostly during Eastertide or shortly after Pentacost, or on some fixed day of a month (18 July, Merseburg; 19 July, Halberstadt, Lxbeck, Meissen; 20 July, Naumberg; cf. Grotefend, "Zeitrechnung", II, 2, 166). Dreves and Blume (Analecta hymnica) have published a large number of rhythmical offices, sequences and hymns for the feast of the Compassion, which show that from the end of the fifteenth century in several dioceses the scope of this feast was widened to commemorate either five dolours, from the imprisonment to the burial of Christ, or seven dolours, extending over the entire life of Mary (cf. XXIV, 122-53; VIII, 51 sq.; X, 79 sq., etc.). Towards the end of the end of the sixteenth century the feast spread over part of the south of Europe; in 1506 it was granted to the nuns of the Annunciation under the title "Spasmi B.M.V.", Monday after Passion Sunday; in 1600 to the Servite nuns of Valencia, "B.M.V. sub pede Crucis", Friday before Palm Sunday. After 1600 it became popular in France and was termed "Dominx N. de Pietate", Friday before Palm Sunday. To this latter date the feast was assigned for the whole German Empire (1674). By a Decree of 22 April 1727, Benedict XIII extended it to the entire Latin Church, under the title "Septem dolorum B.M.V.", although the Office and Mass retain the original character of the feast, the Compassion of Mary at the foot of the Cross. At both Mass and Office the "Stabat Mater" of Giacopone da Todi (1306) is sung.

(2) The second feast was granted to the Servites, 9 June and 15 September, 1668, double with an octave for the third Sunday in September. Its object of the seven dolours of Mary (according to the responsories of Matins: the sorrow

> at the prophecy of Simeon;
> at the flight into Egypt;
> having lost the Holy Child at Jerusalem;
> meeting Jesus on his way to Calvary;
> standing at the foot of the Cross;
> Jesus being taken from the Cross;
> at the burial of Christ.

This feast was extended to Spain (1735); to Tuscany (double of the second class with an octave, 1807). After his return from his exile in France Pius VII extended the feast to the Latin Church (18 September, 1814), major double); it was raised to the rank of a double of the second class, 13 May, 1908.

The Servites celebrate it as a double of the first class with an octave and a vigil. Also in the Passionate Order, at Florence and Granada (N.S. de las Angustias), its rank is double of the first class with an octave.

The hymns which are now used in the Office of this feast were probably composed by the Servite Callisto Palumbella (eighteenth century). On the devotion, cf. Kellner, "Heortology", p. 271. The old title of the "Compassio" is preserved by the Diocese of Hildesheim in a simple feast, Saturday after the octave of Corpus Christi. A feast, "B.M.V. de pietate", with a beautiful medieval office, is kept in honour of the sorrowful mother at Goa in India and Braga in Portugal, on the third Sunday of October; in the ecclesiastical province of Rio de Janeiro in Brazil, last Sunday of May, etc. (cf. the corresponding calendars). A special form of devotion is practised in Spanish-speaking countries under the term of "N.S. de la Soledad", to commemorate the solitude of Mary on Holy Saturday. Its origin goes back to Queen Juana, lamenting the early death of her husband Philip I, King of Spain (1506).

To the oriental churches these feasts are unknown; the Catholic Ruthenians keep a feast of the sorrowful Mother on Friday after the octave of Corpus Christi.

Holweck, Frederick. "Feasts of the Seven Sorrows of the Blessed Virgin Mary." The Catholic Encyclopedia. Vol. 14. New York: Robert Appleton Company, 1912.

Ecclesiastical approbation. Nihil Obstat. July 1, 1912. Remy Lafort, S.T.D., Censor. Imprimatur. +John Cardinal Farley, Archbishop of New York.

Durer Engravings - Christ on the Cross, with the Virgin Mary and John the Theologian 1510 Woodcut 1943.3.3610 VNG. ((PD-US))

Appendix

Indulgences Granted To Those Who Recite The Chaplet Of The Seven Dolours (Sorrows).

This devout prayer, so acceptable to our most holy Sorrowful Mother, and so useful to Christian souls, was propagated throughout the Christian world by these Servants of Mary and it afterwards received much encouragement from Pope Benedict XIII., who, in order to induce the faithful to adopt it more and more, granted by his Brief Redemptoris, of Sept. 26, 1724.

i. An indulgence of DAYS for every Pater noster, and the same for every Hail Mary, to every one who, having Confessed and Communicated, or at least made a firm resolution to Confess, should say this Chaplet in the churches of the Order of the Servants of Mary.

ii. The same indulgence of 200 days to be gained by all who shall say it any where on Fridays, during Lent, and on the Feast and Octave of the Seven Dolours of our Blessed Lady, and -

iii. An indulgence of 100 days, on any other day.

Lastly, the same Pope added –

iv. An indulgence of seven years and seven quarantines to any one who says this Chaplet either alone or in company with others.

Afterwards Pope Clement XII., " that the faithful might often recollect and sympathize with the Dolours of Mary," confirmed by his Bull of Unigeniti, Dec. 12, 1734, the before-named Indulgences, adding also the following:

v. A plenary indulgence and remission of all sins to every one who shall say this Chaplet daily for a month together, and shall then, after Confession and Communion, pray for holy Church, &c.

vi. An indulgence of 100 years, every time it is said, to all who say this chaplet, being truly penitent and having confessed, or having at least made a firm resolution to confess their sins.

vii. An indulgence of 150 years, every Monday, Wednesday, Friday, and Feast of Obligation of the Holy Church, after Confession and Communion.

viii. A plenary indulgence all who say it four times a week, on any one day in the year when, after Confession and Communion, they shall say the said Chaplet of Seven Dolours.

ix. An indulgence of 200 years * also to those who shall say it devoutly after their Confession.

x. An indulgence of ten years to those who keep one of these Chaplets about them, and are in the habit of saying it frequently, every time that, after Confession and Communion, they shall hear Mass, be present at a sermon, accompany the Blessed Sacrament to the sick, make peace between enemies, bring sinners to Confession, &c. &c.; or whenever, saying at the same time seven Pater noster's and seven Hail Mary's, they shall do any spiritual or temporal good work in honour of our Lord Jesus Christ, the Blessed Virgin, or their Patron Saint.

All these Indulgences Mere confirmed by decrees of the S. Congr. of Indulgences issued at the command of Pope Benedict XIV. on January 10, 1711. and Clement XIII.. March 13, 1763. It is, however, requisite, in order to gain these Indulgences, that these Chaplets should be blessed by the Superiors of the Order of the Servants of Mary, or by other priests of the Order deputed by them; and when blessed, they cannot be sold or lent for the purpose of communicating these Indulgences to others, as in that case they would lose the Indulgences. See the above-named Brief of Benedict XIII.

* In some summaries of these Indulgences, and more particularly in that reprinted in Rome in 1518, we find 150 days and a few lines after, 200 days; but in the Bull above named published at the Office of the Reverend Apostolic Chamber in 1135, we find in both places not days but years.

The Raccolta: or Collection of Indulgenced Prayers.With The Appendix of Indulgences Granted by His Holiness Pius IX. From 1856 To 1866.
In particular, see: The Raccolta: Mary Sorrowing.

MATER DOLOROSA.